NEON WORDS

10 Brilliant Ways to Light Up Your Writing

by
Marge Pellegrino & Kay Sather, MA

Magination Press • Washington, DC
American Psychological Association

For Steve & Terry —MP & KS

Books for Kids From the
American Psychological Association
maginationpress.org

Magination Press is a registered trademark of the American Psychological Association. Order books at maginationpress.org, or call 1-800-374-2721.
Artwork & writing samples by authors unless otherwise stated. All other work & quotes used with permission.

Book design and illustrations by Melissa Jane Barrett
Printed by Sonic Media Solutions, Inc., Medford, NY

Library of Congress Cataloging-in-Publication Data
Names: Pellegrino, Marge, author. | Sather, Kay, author.
Title: Neon words : 10 brilliant ways to light up your writing / by Marge Pellegrino & Kay Sather, MA
Description: Washington, DC : Magination Press, 2019. | Includes bibliographical references.
Identifiers: LCCN 2018033817| ISBN 9781433830495 (hardcover) | ISBN 1433830493 (hardcover)
Subjects: LCSH: Authorship--Juvenile literature.
Classification: LCC PN159 .P45 2019 | DDC 808.02--dc23 LC record available at
https://lccn.loc.gov/2018033817

Manufactured in the United States of America
10 9 8 7 6 5 4 3 2 1

CONTENTS

DEAR READER

Grace and I sat on a bench under a tree in Shanghai, China. Spacious lawns reached out in all directions. Sixteen-year-old Grace was interviewing me. She wanted to know how she could become a better writer.

She grew up in an education system that emphasized a straightforward approach to learning and used memorization, drilling, and writing by formula. Not much time was devoted to the creative side—my side—of the street.

She'd never come across activities that involved cutting and pasting, using her drawings or magazine images, or purposely working from random inputs or negative space to draw out creativity.

When I explained some of these approaches, she responded in a direct and gentle way: Why would I do this?

Why?

Before I discovered I could be a writer, I thought writers were magic. What else could account for words that kept me turning pages and devouring stories? They had to be magic if they could create a poem with the power to make me weep, or an article that could get me off my butt and inspire me to jump into something new.

Now that I am a member of the writer clan, I understand that putting pen to paper or cutting out words and moving them around really is magic. Writers work with magic. For me, the process of writing holds that enchantment.

I've thought about Grace since then, wishing I'd told her that there's a way to write that could help her answer her own questions. I could have promised her that in a month, if she started each day writing twenty minutes about whatever she was thinking that morning, she'd see a difference in her writing and in her life—even if she never re-read what she wrote.

I think about other springboard activities I could have shared—those that feed craft and serve as metaphors for bigger, real-life things like transforming emotional trash to treasure or seeking solutions from personal heroes.

Most of all, I wish I had better answered her question: "Why would I do these things?"

As I write these pages, I picture myself handing Grace this book, which offers ways to stretch and grow and have fun with your own ideas and words. I invite you to cross the street with Grace to the imaginative side of writing. You'll find you can work your own magic.

Whether you want to be a writer, or just want to explore what it's like to create with language, you'll discover that playing with words can help you be more present in your life—and best of all, it's lots of fun.

Xie xie, thank you, Grace!

Marge Pellegrino (MP)

I wish I'd had this book when I was younger. I hoped I would become a writer, but I didn't know where to start. If my teacher gave me a writing assignment, like a book review or a research paper, I knew exactly what to do, and I enjoyed the writing. But on my own I was clueless. Exactly how would I become a writer? Would I have to look for an employer who would tell me what to write? If I wrote what I wanted, on my own time, how would I pay for my food and shelter? It wasn't until I'd already started out on a different career that I got an assignment from a magazine and finally began to write.

Don't wait that long! This book is full of ideas for getting your writing revved up and flying. It's not some boring instruction manual with a title like, "How to Become a Writer." It's a book that will illuminate the writer in you. By using the tools and activities here, you'll connect the word-organizing part of your brain with your free-ranging imagination—and you'll love what you've captured on the page. It's an exciting, confidence-boosting, enlightening, and deeply satisfying experience. It's how writers are born.

So now you can get started on your path. It will be your own unique path, no one else's. This book is your trailhead.

Kay Sather (KS)

EXPRESSIVE WRITING
—THE KIND YOU'LL

Writing about your inner life helps you:

- Loosen up your prose so it sparkles like poetry! Even if you aren't interested in writing poems, you can use these activities to give your writing the buoyancy and surprising twists that will keep your readers reading. Your writing will pop off the page if you let it. It will fly to the moon!
- Master your writing at school and have fun doing it! Fun happens when you find the material that matters to you.
- Get healthy! Researchers have shown that people who write about emotional upheavals require fewer doctor visits and are generally healthier.
- Combat depression! Writing a gratitude journal helps with mood. Expressing yourself lets you ditch your stress for a while. It gives you a break, and sometimes even an escape from the rough parts of your life.
- Build your brain! Some people think best with words, music, movement, or by talking with others. Some use logic, art, or being alone to kickstart their thinking. *Neon Words* invites you to think in a variety of ways, which will result in stronger writing and a smarter you!

DO HERE—
HAS MANY BENEFITS.

This book is a little bit different from other writing books that only ask you to write. Each chapter has three dynamic sections:

- *Strengthen Your Words*: tools that can be used repeatedly to improve and enrich your writing. They might help you overcome some personal writing challenges.
- *Honor Your Words*: physical ways to hold your words and show them respect. This will give your words and ideas weight, making them touchable, visible, and beautiful. Your words can become a gift—to yourself or someone else—and in a sense, they're published.
- *Play With Your Words*: activities that will push you to generate meaningful content. These are inspiring for writers who feel like they have nothing to say.

Just remember: You're the boss. These pages hold only suggestions. So, improvise! Use the ideas to get yourself started. Feel free to begin with any tool, activity, or physical honoring of your words. We've put them in a logical order, but you don't have to follow it. Be the boss of your writing. Get ready to be surprised by where your words will take you.

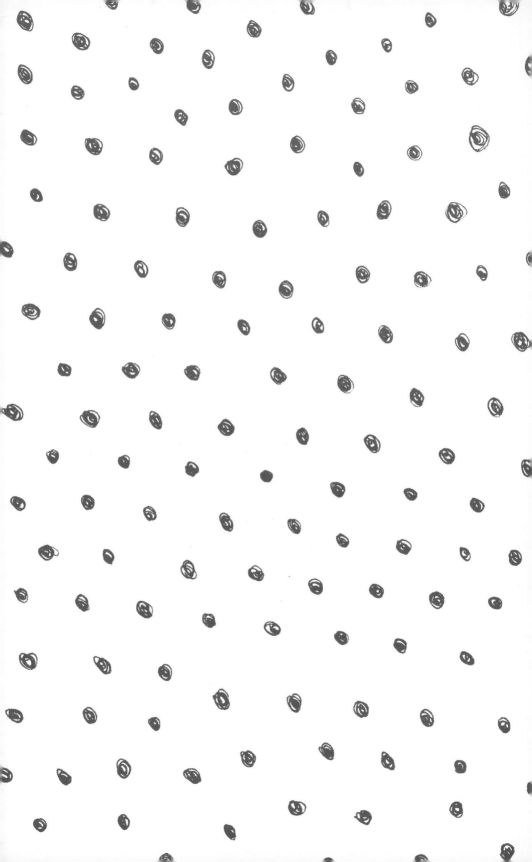

CHAPTER

Make It Personal

PERSONALIZED JOURNAL

Explore your identity through a personalized journal and a self-portrait.

Throughout *Neon Words* we share lots of ways writing can make you stronger, and many include using a journal. Whether you create different journals for different projects, or you put all your writing adventures into one journal, you can claim it as a receptacle of your thoughts.

Choose a journal that's lined or not lined, hardcover, spiral-bound or softcover. It doesn't need to be new. It could be an old notebook with usable pages, even ones you could paint over or use as a jumping-off point. Check a thrift store. Check your closet.

Whichever you choose, consider personalizing the cover of your journal by collaging images from magazines or your own artwork. You could use stickers or stick-on letters or shapes. Try decorating with colored tapes, glitter paint, or fabric. In some way, visually claim the cover. If you date the inside cover and each day's entries, you'll always know when you wrote them.

On the inside cover or the cover itself, consider writing or collaging an intention, such as: "Take care of MYSELF" or "Make a difference!" It could be a phrase that will remind you what you hope to achieve while using the journal, or a goal you'll reach before the pages are filled, like "Write three poems I'll be proud to share." Because the cover and inside cover of your journal are places you'll look at frequently, the intention will be strengthened in your mind—even unconsciously.

On Zines

If you find that you love the visual design aspect of your journal, you might be someone who would enjoy producing and sharing your own (maga)zine. Carlee Ricketts did it when she was 15—we were subscribers and looked forward to each issue that arrived in the mail. Here's what she says about her inspiration (personal communication, 2018):

"I was homeschooled and very thin-skinned—the kind of girl too wrapped up in daydreams to have felt anything but lonely most of the time. Except in pages. Pages and pages of all sorts of words and stories.

It will still be a couple decades before I've percolated a book, but I've written poems for years. The Weetzie Bat series by Francesca Lia Block was a favorite kind of modern and alternative fairy tale that eventually my adult life would resemble. In my endless library loitering, I found out she had co-authored a non-fiction book about zines! Xeroxed and handcrafted magazines of all kinds! Printed pirate radio! I didn't know how to get to a punk rock show, and I didn't know my favorite songs yet, but I was 15 and I knew enough to fill a diary-like zine every few months, and that was a revolution.

The words I've written and the words I don't have time for now and the words I feel building everyday are so magic it's stupid. The words that I read every day from old and new voices, both renowned and unknown, are the blood of our human community."

CONSCIOUS BREATHING

Thinking about your breathing keeps your mind from wandering and prepares you to focus on writing.

There are many ways to do the ancient practice of deliberate breathing, which comes to us from India. The version outlined below is inspired by ocean waves breaking on the shore and then receding. You can do it anywhere, in any position—sitting, lying, or standing.

Inhale deeply through your nose.

Hold your breath for five seconds at the "top."

Exhale slowly to empty your lungs.

Pause again for a count of five at the "bottom."

Repeat for five breaths.

This exercise is really relaxing, especially in the pause at the end of the exhale.

SIMILE SELF-PORTRAIT

Similes, as you may know, are phrases that compare one thing to another using "like" or "as." For example: My toes are little like peanuts. Or: I'm as tall as a tree. (Variation: I'm tall as a tree.)

This springboard activity is a three-for-one. You'll end up with a unique self-portrait, two simile-inspired poems, and a clearer idea of metaphors.

Begin by drawing yourself. Use your non-dominant hand if you'd like to push your usual visual reality. Detailed or spare, black and white or color—it's up to you. Now attach some similes to different parts of yourself.

Check out this self-portrait by artist and writer Terry Owen and the similes he attached to it:

Your similes don't have to follow the pattern "My ___ is like a ___." You could also use active verbs like curl, light, and bend (see Marge's list below).

My hair curls like a slow river.
My hair is brown, like the bark of a tree.
My brain is as curious as a monkey's.
My smile lights up my face like a light bulb flipped on.
My voice is as smooth as a song.
My heart is warm, like dinner rolls fresh out of the oven.
My knees bend like a hinge.
My hands can be as strong as superglue or as gentle as a lamb.
My legs run as fast as the wind over an airplane wing.

Now type out your similes and then enlarge them, either by enlarging the type on the computer or with a copy machine. Or forget the typing and just rewrite them bigger, so they're easy to cut out and move around. You won't need all the words. Choose the ones you consider strong.

Once you've written and cut out your favorite words, you're ready to play with syntax—that is, to manipulate their order. The more you challenge the common order of things the better. When you drop the "like" and "as" you're creating metaphor.

As you find word combinations you like, set them aside. Move the lines and phrases around to find an order that feels right. At this point, you can add words that make it complete before you glue them down.

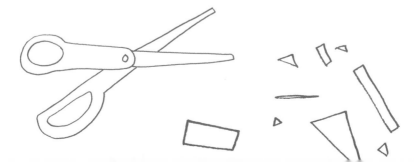

Here's the imaginative poem pulled from Terry's self-portrait:

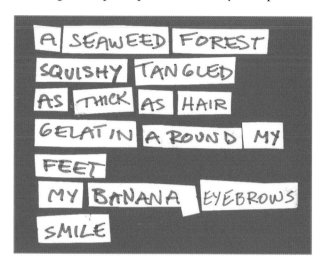

> A SEAWEED FOREST
> SQUISHY TANGLED
> AS THICK AS HAIR
> GELATIN AROUND MY
> FEET
> MY BANANA EYEBROWS
> SMILE

This activity also presents an opportunity to play with alliteration—to weave in an echo, a repetition of sound, as in "brown like bark" or "smooth as a song" or "strong like super glue."

Finally, here's the poem Marge found in her similes:

With My Bark-Brown Hair

and light-switch smile,
my monkey brain
thinks in slow curls
curious

With knees hinged
and wind-fast legs
my feet move me
swift

Watch how far I'll go!
– MP

CHAPTER

2

Remember
the Details

LISTING ☆ ☆ ☆

Using listing as your tool, harvest captivating details from the rich well of memory.

Listing is sweet and simple but powerful. Ask successful people; you'll find they use lists as springboards to action.

Lists are also the simplest way to get your brain churning. Listing is quick, down, and dirty. It's a way to brainstorm solutions and possibilities. Lists help you nail down the points you want to make in an essay, or, for that matter, what you want to cover in any writing. For example, if you want to write a thank-you note, or a toast to honor someone, a list will ensure you don't miss an important detail.

What kind of list do you want to write? For ideas, check out this list of lists! You could write a list about:

- People—family . . . friends . . . teachers . . . presidents . . . celebrities
- Sounds—musical . . . natural . . . urban
- Food—styles of cooking . . . main courses . . . snacks . . . places to eat
- Smells—unpleasant . . . pleasant . . . childhood . . . holiday
- Songs—musical instruments . . . singers . . . genres
- Hobbies—gardening . . . hiking . . . reading . . . singing . . . biking
- Animals—pets . . . breeds of dogs . . . endangered . . . water-dwelling
- Things that inspire you
- Best/worst moments
- Things that make you laugh or cry
- Landscapes and places
- Games—sports . . . electronic . . . board . . . cards
- Clothing—hats . . . footwear . . . seasonal . . . styles
- Books—characters (fictional, real) . . . authors . . . to read . . . best-ever stories
- Events—celebrations (kinds of parties) . . . cultural variations
- Weather

- *Things you love*
- *Things you want to accomplish or master*

In some of the activities that follow, you'll have a chance to list. Use single words or whole phrases. You could write the list in a column, leaving space to the right for expanding your ideas later. You can give yourself even more room by leaving space between the lines, too.

To try out this tool now, choose a topic for the list. Jot down the list, then read it over, circling the ideas that hold the most power or potential. Then choose one idea to expand on, and write your short story, essay, poem, or some other piece (it might inspire another list!).

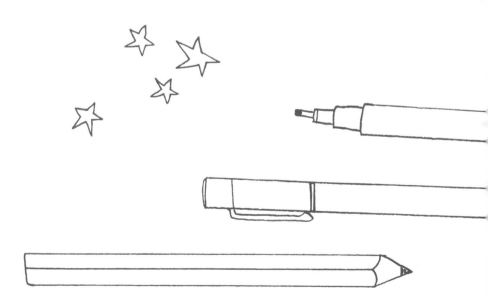

SHAPE POEMS

Shape poems combine words and images. They stretch your spatial and linguistic smarts. The result can enhance the meaning of your thoughts and feelings.

A.

when avid cats appear nearby / the birds do / from the ground explode / into the sky, beaks filled with seeds! / Quick-beating hearts, wings bearing loads

There are two basic kinds of shape poems. In one, the list of words or the poem traces the outline of the shape (A, from Terry Owen), and in the other, they fill it in (B, from KS).

Now try it! For (A), sketch a simple outline of your object. Make your poem fit this shape by varying the size of your letters to make the text fit the outline. With (B), fill in the shape with your poem, again using different letter sizes until it fits. You can even try a simple variation of (B) by filling in your shape poem with single letters or words that go with the shape (such as repeating the word "ear" to form the shape of a dog's ear).

B.

I AM DRAWN TO YOU LIKE A MOTH TO A FLAME. LUCKILY THE WIND BLOWS IT OUT BEFORE I GET TOO CLOSE. WHAT DOES THAT MEAN?

If you need more inspiration, search for "shape poems" or "famous shape poems" on the Internet. You'll find some wonderful examples.

MINING MEMORIES

Don't tell me the moon is shining;
show me the glint of light on broken glass.
—Anton Chekhov

Remembering when you were younger often opens you up to a time when you were immersed in play, wonder, discovery, and creativity. But with this exercise, you can also remember details of this morning—what you had for breakfast, the sounds outside your window, things you were looking forward to.

Here you'll play with a list poem. A true list poem has a considered order and a last line that either reflects the intention of your list, or lifts and shifts its meaning.

Before you write your own, read the following list poem by Joe Brainard:

I Remember

I remember the only time I ever saw my mother cry. I
    was eating apricot pie.
I remember how much I used to stutter.
I remember the first time I saw television. Lucille Ball
    was taking ballet lessons.
I remember Aunt Cleora who lived in Hollywood. Every
    year for Christmas she sent my brother and me a
    joint present of one book.
I remember a very poor boy who had to wear his sister's
    blouses to school.
I remember shower curtains with angel fish on them.
I remember very old people when I was very young.
    Their houses smelled funny.
I remember daydreams of being a singer all alone on a
    big stage with no scenery, just one spotlight on me,

singing my heart out, and moving my audience to
total tears of love and affection.

I remember waking up somewhere once and there was a
horse staring me in the face.

I remember saying "thank you" in reply to "thank you"
and then the other person doesn't know what to say.

I remember how embarrassed I was when other children
cried.

I remember one very hot summer day I put ice cubes in
my aquarium and all the fish died.

I remember not understanding why people on the other
side of the world didn't fall off.

Where does the poem really pop for you? Not sure? Read this watered-down version and notice what's missing.

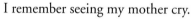

I Remember (Apologies to Joe Brainard)

I remember seeing my mother cry.

I remember stuttering.

I remember seeing television.

I remember Aunt Cleora sending me a present.

I remember a poor kid from school.

I remember the shower curtain.

I remember people's houses smelled.

I remember daydreaming about being a performer.

I remember seeing a horse stare at me.

I remember saying "thank you" to a "thank you."

I remember seeing other children cry.

I remember killing my fish.

I remember not understanding so much.

If you think the first version of the poem is richer, we're with you! What's the primary difference you noticed between the first and the second?

It's a lack of detail. It's missing what gives writing a crispness and depth. This includes sensory and emotional detail. For example, what kind of fish decorated the shower curtains? (Visual.) What was memorable about your mother crying? (Emotional.)

Any line of Joe Brainard's poem, if its components are examined and labeled, can inspire a line of your own. Below are some of the poem's lines followed by categories you might springboard from:

> I remember the only time I ever saw my mother cry. I
>   was eating apricot pie.
> *Unique event, family, sadness, food, taste.*

> I remember how much I used to stutter.
> *Embarrassment, sense of hearing.*

> I remember one very hot summer day I put ice cubes in
>   my aquarium and all the fish died.
> *Unintended consequence, tactile sense.*

> I remember very old people when I was very young.
>   Their houses smelled funny.
> *Sense of smell, comparison—young and old.*

> I remember not understanding why people on the other
>   side of the world didn't fall off.
> *Puzzlement, an aha! moment.*

Other categories you might find in the poem are: surprise, daydreaming, injustice, colors and images, weather, animals, love, song, and place.

Brainard also includes qualifiers such as "the only time" and "the first time." These are the kind of details you don't want to forget in your writing!

Before you begin to collect your own strong details, find some index cards (or make your own out of paper) and write one "I remember" line of your own on each card. Now order the cards until you're pleased with the result.

You can use the categories to cue your own poem. Example:

> I remember my mother throwing volume "N" from the
> encyclopedia across the room at my brother and
> breaking the coffee table. Glass everywhere.
> I remember seeing people cry and dance on television
> when Nelson Mandela died.
> I remember the first time I fought with my little
> brother and he won.

If these cues aren't producing the details you want, try tapping into your body's memories. Take a break from the writing to do a cartwheel, a couple of yoga poses, or some dance moves. Listen to music from your past or look through photos from childhood or family photos from back in the day. Imagine yourself back in a wild place you once visited. Write down what pops into your head and make a poem.

When you're done, go back and consider places where you could add:

- Similes where they might make your line sparkle.
- Alliteration (words that repeat the same sound) to make a line resonate.
- Details that show instead of tell, as in Chekhov's phrase, "glint of light on broken glass."
- Repetition. Repeating the phrase "I Remember" gives the poem a rhythm. Try repeating other words like "lots and lots and lots of love"—the last line of the following "Shanghai, I Remember" poem, written collaboratively by teens at Shanghai High School in China.

Shanghai, I Remember

I remember the first time I laid eyes on my baby brother
and how he looked so fragile and vulnerable.
I remember leaves dancing to the ground as I walked
through autumn zephyrs.
I remember putting my dog on the slide, how scared he
was, and how he avenged me by peeing.
I remember sitting on my grandfather's strong shoulders,
clinging for dear life onto fistfuls of his hair.
I remember being excited when I saw a shooting star flash
across the night sky. I made a wish, only to realize that
it was just a bird.
I remember when my older brother shoved me into a
deep dense pool. Once I got up, I attacked him.
Pow! I heard the water splash and leapt out of the
pool.
I remember the crooked-eared cat stalking across the
manicured lawns, ignoring the long-tailed jay's
attacks.
I remember the painful, perplexed look on my girlfriend's
face when she bit into the piping-hot dumpling, our
first meal on Baise.
I remember my small self and the rush of curiosity as
I glared into my seeping gash from the fall off the
bike.
I remember walking on the sunny side of the storm,
looking back, and seeing a whole city covered with
pitch black clouds and feeling like I had no worries
in the world. Such naiveté.
I remember lots and lots and lots of love.

Building your list poem around a single word.

Another approach to writing a list poem is to describe an emotion by listing as many phrases and images as you can to express or illustrate the emotion.

What do you think the emotion behind this short list poem might be?

A Single Shoe on the Side of the Road

A nail sticking out of a bare wall
A car alone in a parking lot with the trunk open
An empty chair pulled out from a table
A phone that rings and rings and rings
Words swallowed
Eyes averted
— MP

Instead of an emotion you could describe your bedroom, your mother, the Universe . . . anything that suggests a list will work.

Building your poem around a list of new words.

If you're taking a language class or reading above your comfort level, look up the words you don't understand and use them to write a list poem. It's crazy fun and great for expanding your vocabulary!

Double-Duty Dictionary

Gayle Brandeis, a Bellwether Prize-winning author, used the dictionary to inspire her poetry. Every day for two months, she randomly chose a word from the dictionary and incorporated that word into a poem. Gayle says, "The dictionary is both a tool chest and a treasure chest for writers; think of all the amazing words it holds, words we can pull out and combine to create something brand new. I've been writing dictionary poems off and on for over ten years now—it's still my favorite way to get my creative juices flowing, to reignite my love of language" (personal communication, 2018). Her work using that strategy turned into the book *Dictionary Poems*, published by Pudding House Publications.

Chekhov, A. (n.d.). [Quote]. Retrieved from: https://quoteinvestigator.com/2013/07/30/moon-glint/

Padgett, R. (2012). *Collected writings of Joe Brainard*. New York, NY: Library of America.

CHAPTER 3

Switch It Up

SIMPLE-8 BINDING

Borrow and remix your way to original writing and discovery.

Now we'll make a simple journal or booklet for your writing that you can bind yourself by sewing the binding in the shape of an 8.

What you'll need:

- Cover stock or heavier-weight paper, 8 ½ inches by 11 inches. (You can use lighter weight paper, but collaging with liquid glue will ripple your cover—use a glue stick.)
- Plain paper, 8 ½ inches by 11 inches. This will provide the inside of the journal. One page (the minimum) will provide you with four writing surfaces. Using more than three pages may challenge the strength of your needle and will push the inside pages out farther than the cover.
- Needle. A regular needle will work, but a book-binding needle is preferable because it's uniformly thick from eye to point. Look for one at a craft store.
- Thread. This should be heavier than regular sewing thread. Linen is best because it won't stretch. Multi-strand embroidery thread works—use as many strands as will fit in your needle.

Optional:

- Beads. You can string beads or other embellishments along the spine, or on the ends of the binding tails, as long as the needle will fit through the bead's hole.
- Beeswax. Running thread through beeswax makes it easier to thread the needle. Also, when you finish the binding, your knot will hold better.
- Collage material and glue.

Directions:

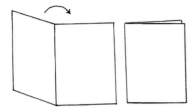

1. Fold the cover stock and paper in half, either the skinny way (hot dog fold) or the fat way (hamburger fold).

2. Cut your thread to approximately 26 inches (hot dog fold) or 20 inches (hamburger fold, shown here).

3. Thread your needle, leaving the ends unknotted.

4. Unfold your book-to-be. Poke a hole through the center of the outside fold from the cover through the pages. This will be the meeting point of the eight.

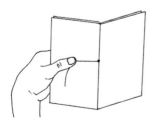

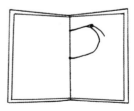

5. Pull the thread through the hole, leaving a five-inch tail. To avoid pulling it all the way through, hold the end of the string against the paper with your free thumb.

6. Now make the second hole about an inch from one end of the fold. This time you'll be going from the inside to the outside.

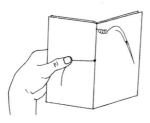

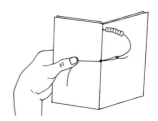

7. String any beads for the first half of the spine.

8. Poke your needle back into the middle hole (the first one you made). You'll be going back inside. Avoid stabbing the thread that's already there. (If you do stab the thread it's not the end of the world, but it will make it more challenging to adjust the thread later.) This will complete the top loop of the 8.

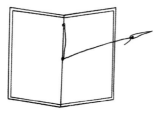

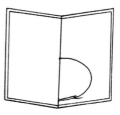

9. Pull the string tight without pulling it all the way through (keep pinching that tail!).

10. Make the next hole about an inch from the other end of the fold and pull the thread back out.

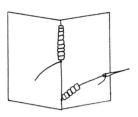 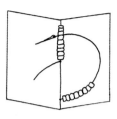

11. Add any beads or embellishments for the other half of the spine.

12. Bring the needle under the thread of the first segment of the figure 8.

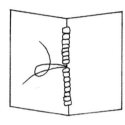 

13. Tie a double knot with the two tails. If you'd like more beads on the tails, add them now! You could use one bead as the knot to hold the others on, or make your knot big enough (using multiple knots) to keep the beads in place.

14. You're ready to write!

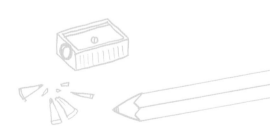

SYNTAX SWITCH-UP

Noun + verb + object. Noun + verb + object. BORING!

After a while, the expected order of words can feel monotonous. Shaking up that order and playing with syntax is the easiest way to loosen up (like we did in the simile self-portrait in Chapter One). Stretch your writing as you discover new, unexpected ways words might go together. For example, you could write down or print out "The flower is a pink rose," and cut the words apart. Moving them around, you might get:

> The pink flower is a rose.
> Pink is a rose. (You've dropped two words.)
> Pink rose, flower! (Flower becomes a verb—the statement becomes a command.)
> Rose, the flower is pink. (Talking to a person named Rose.)
> The flower rose pink. (Is it floating? Maybe!)
> A pink flower rose. (Now rose becomes a verb.)

Remember, you're the boss. Feel free to change the tense, the number, the article, or add a different pronoun.

> My pink roses flower. (Possession and more than one rose.)

FOUND POEMS

Found poems rock! People love creating them. Found poems feel fresh and cutting-edge, but they actually came from the surrealist movement, also referred to as Dadaism, of almost a hundred years ago. The movement included both visual and literary artists. Probably its most famous visual artist was Salvador Dalí, best known for his paintings of melting clocks.

There are many ways to "find" a poem. Here are six strategies.

1. Cut ten to thirty words and phrases from flyers, magazines, or newspapers. Set them on a large piece of paper. Move them around until you find a poem, a statement, or a line that you love. You can save any leftover words for another poem or collage.

2. You can also use your own words as source material. Choose a favorite story you've written, or write one on a topic that interests you. Now underline the heartfelt phrases and sentences. Use these as lines for your poem, adding and subtracting words as needed. On the next page is a story by Indrawati D., a 17-year-old from Nepal, and the poem she pulled from it. (The lines she ultimately used for the poem are indicated in bold face in the story.)

My Bro and Me

I didn't remember that I pushed my brother down the stairs when I was a child, so I was really frightened when my mom told me about it. I was five years old and my brother was only three. My grandparents' house was surrounded by a flower garden and a lot of trees and mountains. It was early and I just woke up and took a shower. My brother was sitting on the stairs drinking milk and eating breakfast. I was also watching the birds and enjoying the peaceful environment. My brother was teasing me, but I was quiet because I really admired and enjoyed the cool romantic atmosphere. Suddenly he made me mad, so I pushed him from the stairs and then grabbed my sandals and hurried downstairs. My grandmother turned to him and asked "what happened to you?" He burst out crying. So my grandmother knew it was me. I was really afraid because I thought they might ask me why I would do that. Next, they took him to the hospital and brought him back at night. Now my **mom asked me many questions, but I didn't have any answers to them. I couldn't look into her face and I just looked down at the floor.** I don't remember what happened next. I know that my mom still had many questions. Now I feel remorse for everything that happened and I usually choose to behave like a mature person. I promised I would never repeat such a mistake. I even give him medicines and am nice to everyone. **Mom tells us there is a time and place where kids learn. My brother nods and says: "Okay but don't repeat that, my lovely sister."** So I look at the sky and say, "Thank God." That was a big part of my learning. Now I know how to be honest and live in peace with my family.

Here's the poem that was freed from the page:

Mom Asked Me Many Questions

But I didn't have any answers to them.
I couldn't look into her face
I just looked down at the floor…
Mom tells us there is a time
and place where kids learn.
My brother nods and says:
"Okay, but don't repeat that, my lovely sister."

3. Another way to "find" a poem is to use a page from your journal. You can add an element of randomness by folding the page in half the skinny way. Circle the words and phrases that speak to you the loudest.

4. Cut out an illustration from a magazine or old calendar, or draw something yourself. *Ekphrasis* is a kind of writing—usually poetry—where the writer describes a work of art (usually a visual piece). What's happening in the image? What details makes you say that? What else do you see? On paper or labels, write down phrases the image inspires. Cut those words out and use them to create a found poem. The following poem was inspired by the image next to it. What's happening in the image on the next page?

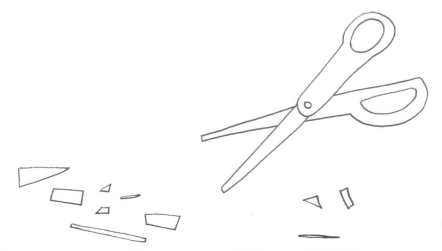

Original art by Kay Sather

Build a Word Collection

In *Poemcrazy*, author Susan G. Wooldridge talks about how she carries around tickets for writing down words that grab her attention. Try carrying scraps of paper or a small pack of sticky notes. Jot down interesting words you overhear, copy them from a bulletin board at a coffee shop, or find them on billboards, signs, even plant labels in a park. Arrange the words you collect to make a poem for your closet door, or anywhere else you might want to leave a poem.

Woolridge, S. G. (1997). *Poemcrazy: Freeing your life with words*. New York, NY: Three Rivers Press.

Galaxy Heat

Discover the summer moon
as night-sky wings
flutter

Prickly desert
blooms desire
hope rises full

The light cycle
pollinates, reproduces,
grows back

Craters in delicate
shadows
white desert illuminated

Spiny-sharp ridges
hold round blooms
that open at dusk
like budding stars
bright
fragrant

Bats fly wide
eclipsing
the hot night
pollinating the cold moon
petals rising
desire flutters

Cereus delight

— MP & KS

5. Copy out a poem from a poet you love. Copying is not a robotic task; you'll learn something about how the poet constructed the poem before you deconstruct it. Cut out the words and see what else you might say using some of those same words. Make your own rules! Will you separate compound words? Do you want to use every word? Do you want to choose just the top ten words? Will you allow yourself to use homonyms, like changing "there" to "their"? Or add some words of your own to the mix? Do you want to pull lines from different poems?

You could also pull lines from other sources, such as book titles, song lyrics, stories, or plays. Use your material in whatever way works for you!

Too nice girl
Why are you SO scared?
Did you hear?
NOBODY"S PERFECT.
Be Calm.
Grow Grateful.
Dream it!
Bounce Back.

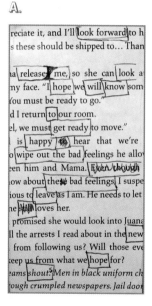PLAY

6. Select! Begin by choosing a published text, a page from your journal, or something in the recycle pile. Circle the words you'd like to keep (A). As you do this, you'll also be eliminating words that don't work for you, just as a sculptor chips away at stone or carves away clay. By using a pen or pencil to cross out words and phrases, you'll make something entirely new—a story or poem. This technique is sometimes called a "blackout" approach (B).

Another option is to use the unwanted text as a field for doodling, coloring, or painting—creating art that showcases your chosen words (C).

A.

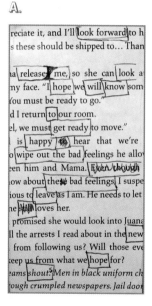

B.

C.

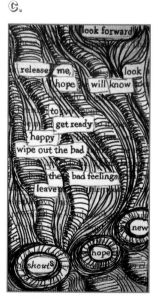

CHAPTER 4

Look Who's Talking

HAIKU HOLDER

*Play with voices. Listen for which ones
hold power, and let the characters speak!*

This embellished mini-folder can also hold any short poem, story, greeting, or even your six-word memoir. See how much content the legendary six-word 'short story' below, apocryphally attributed to Ernest Hemmingway, holds:

> For sale: baby shoes, never worn.

Here are two lesser-known examples:

> Dirt yard, add water, adobe house. (Memoir, KS)
> Book bonkers, word wild, library lunatic! (Memoir, MP)

You can also find examples online by searching for "six-word memoirs."

Save and recycle your coffee-cup sleeves! If you make your own hot beverages or tend to drink out of a real cup (good for you!), ask someone else to save some for you.

What you'll need:

- Coffee sleeve
- Narrow ribbon at least 15 inches long
- Utility knife or other sharp blade
- Paint or collage material and glue

Directions:

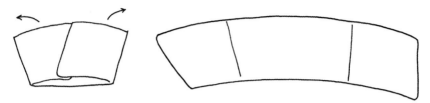

1. Gently pry apart the glued ends of the sleeve. If it seems about to tear, loosen the glue with heat from the sun or from your microwave (no more than 10 seconds).

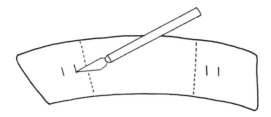

2. Skip this step if your coffee holders already have holes in them. If not, use your knife or blade to make two pairs of slits wide enough for your ribbon. Each pair of slits (forming two tabs) should be close to their respective ends of the coffee sleeve. You need to be able to see both tabs when the sleeve is closed.

3. Thread your ribbon so it runs around the outside of your holder, with each end going through a tab. The advertising should be on the inside (which was the outside when it was part of the cup).

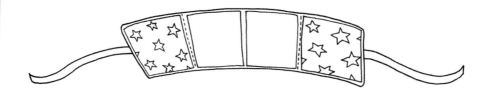

4. Cover the advertising with paint or a collage. Or use blank paper for more writing space. Now it's ready for your message.

5. After you've written your poetry or greeting, close the side flaps and tie off the ribbon. Make a bow and it's a gift — to yourself or someone else.

A haiku could be just the right content for your holder. The haiku is an ancient Japanese form of poetry, traditionally consisting of three lines. The first line has five syllables, the second seven, and the last five. At the end of the first or second line, the haiku shifts—providing a turning point or a moment of surprise.

Basho, an honored Japanese haiku poet, wrote in the 1600s, and people today still look to his poems for inspiration. One, translated for us by our friend Larry Hammer, is printed below.

> In-between the waves—
> mingled with the small seashells
> bush-clover debris.

A traditional haiku always has nature as its topic. If you write about *human* nature, your haiku becomes a senryu. Example:

> Two friends together
> wrestle words with the hope they
> will inspire others.
> —MP & KS

Here's another interesting option for the inside of your holder. Beat poet Allen Ginsberg felt that haiku didn't work very well in English, so he would write a single 17-syllable sentence called an "American Sentence." Here's an example by Juanita Havill:

> Writing these words makes me sad; my heart-friend with
> the tailless wag is gone.

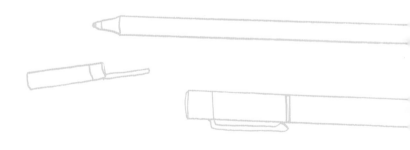

DIALOGUE

Dialogue helps you "show" instead of "tell"—always a writer's goal. Good dialogue reports conversation in a way that reveals character, humor, emotion, and/or a narrative twist. It breaks up the narrative and brings the reader into a more sharply-drawn scene.

Except for the stage notes and the occasional soliloquy (character speaking to themselves), plays are pretty much all dialogue. Here's an example from Shakespeare's *A Midsummer Night's Dream*:

> Bottom: Are we all met?
>
> Quince: Pat, pat; and here is a marvellous convenient
>   place for our rehearsal. This green plot shall be our
>   stage, this hawthorn brake our tiring-house; and we
>   will do it in action, as we will do it before the duke.
>
> Bottom: Peter Quince,—
>
> Quince: What say'st thou, bully Bottom?
>
> Bottom: There are things in this comedy of Pyramus and
>   Thisby that will never please. First, Pyramus must
>   draw a sword to kill himself; which the ladies cannot
>   abide. How answer you that?
>
> Snout: By'r lakin, a parlous fear.
>
> Starveling: I believe you must leave the killing out, when
>   all is done.
>
> Bottom: Not a whit: I have a device to make all well . . .

Note that this two-person dialogue is joined by two others as it progresses. It's still called a dialogue!

Good dialogue is never an information dump. Don't use dialogue to get across narrative facts. Instead, use it in a way that's natural to conversation. The following is an example of awkwardness due to an info-dump:

"You're kidding! This is the pond?" I asked. "How can they call it that? It's smaller than a bathtub, sitting here at the edge of the patio, under steps that go nowhere."

"Xeriscaping," Mom said. "Low water use. But lush, don't you think?"

Some details of the scene would be better included in a description:

"You're kidding! This is the pond?" I asked.

The pond, if it could be called that, was smaller than a bathtub. It sat at the edge of the patio, under a staircase that led up to the blank side of a building. The stairway wasn't entirely useless, though, as each step held lush-looking potted plants.

"Xeriscaping," Mom said. "Low water use."

Of course, the best examples of great dialogue can be the ones you come across in your favorite books! Notice them as you read.

Be sure to notice use of quotation marks, other punctuation, line breaks, attributions (who said what, as well as how they said it). Some writers are now playing with different dialogue formats, such as dropping quotation marks altogether. Decide what you like!

Your assignment here, if you choose to accept it, is to write a scene with only dialogue. Create a conversation with two characters. It could be:

Someone new to the city talking with a native
Someone talking with a person from the past
An extraterrestrial asking for directions or instructions
Two animals whose paths cross
Your pet talking with you

Read your piece out loud. Feel the words in your throat, hear them in your ears. This attention to literal speech will help you build a distinctive voice, critical for anything you write.

POINT OF VIEW

Who's talking in your story or poem? It doesn't have to be a person or even a living being. It could be an artifact from your room, a poster at the movie theater, a tree stump, or a car. In your imagination, anyone or anything can talk. Everything has potential for playing with point-of-view.

1. Choose your character. For example, *flowers*.

2. Write a line about it (third person): *Flowers are beautiful.*

3. Write a line that talks to it (second person). You decide if you're talking as a friend, foe, or neutral acquaintance—maybe a stranger just happening upon it:

   Flower, thanks for blooming for me today.
   Flower, you stabbed me—what's that about?
   Flower, you look delicate.
   What a surprise you are, Flower!

4. Write a line as though you were it (first person). *I grew, just for you.*

5. Read the lines out loud. Each line is a different speaker, so involve your voice. Be over-the-top dramatic. Just for fun, watch Sarah Jones do her one-woman show of very distinct voices of characters from her neighborhood (visit ted.com, and search for "A one-woman global village").

6. Decide which of the lines you wrote sounds most powerful and continue writing your scene, story, or poem from that point of view. Or write from all three points of view, as Marge does in the following examples.

About Flowers

Flowers ask so little
a drink of clear water
sunshine
a place to cling to the earth.
So little for what they give
vibrant color
enticing perfume
soft beauty that
feeds the soul.

Here, she becomes a friend of the flower:

Hey flower

you're gonna like
these writers.
Check them out!
They're poem makers
story creators.
They light up the room
with their neon words.

Then she becomes the flower itself:

I reach toward the sun

its warmth feeds me
like the earth and rain

touch my baby-soft petals
hear me whisper

smell my thin-scent trail
don't let my thorns
pierce your finger

cut me for your rituals
hand me to your mother
throw me into the open grave
sprinkle my petals at the wedding
let me feed your spirit

De Groot, J. (1989). *Papa: A play based on the legendary lives of Ernest Hemingway*. Boise, ID: Boise State University.

Jones, S. (2009, February). *Sarah Jones, TED2009: A one-woman global village* [Video file]. Retrieved from: https://www.ted.com/talks/sarah_jones_as_a_one_woman_global_village?language=en

Shakespeare, W. (n.d.). *A midsummer night's dream*. Retrieved from: https://www.opensourceshakespeare. org/views/plays/playmenu.php?WorkID=midsummer (Original work published 1959)

Smith, L. & Fershleiser, R. (2008). *Not quite what I was planning: Six-word memoirs by writers famous and obscure*. New York, NY: Harper Perennial.

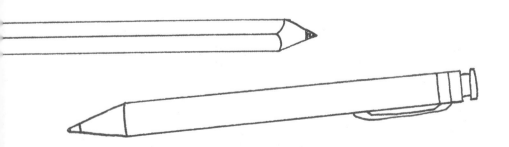

CHAPTER

5

The Antagonist

THREE-SPREAD BOOK

What happens when you take the oppositional point of view?

All you need is a piece of paper and a pair of scissors. And, as a bonus, this book is reversible! Turn it inside out to realize its full potential. You can write about one topic—for example, the events of your day—then open it up, and refold so that the day story will be on the inside. With the new outside, write about a contrasting topic like what happened the following night.

Directions:

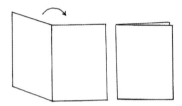

1. Fold a piece of paper (any size) in half using the "hamburger" fold rather than the "hot dog" fold. You now have two layers. If you want to make sure your crease is sharp, open and refold in the opposite direction.

2. As a folded sheet, make another hamburger fold and re-crease as above. Now there are four layers.

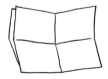

3. Fold again and re-crease. This will give you eight layers and the piece you hold will be ⅛ the size of your original sheet.

4. Open to the first fold. You'll have two layers, and you'll see a creased cross in the paper.

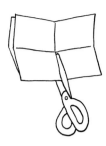

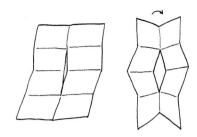

5. Make a cut from the folded edge to the center of the cross.

6. Now open the page completely, and this time, make a hot dog fold. Hold your paper so the center fold points out, not inward. (If they do turn inward, open the sheet up and make the hot dog fold in the other direction.)

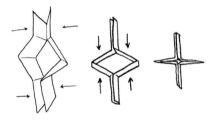

7. Holding the ends, move your hands together a few inches and look for the diamond that will form in the middle. Keep moving your hands together until the folds touch. You'll form an X.

8. Catch two flaps in each hand, and fold in half again.

Voila! You have a three-spread book ready for your words, illustrations, story, or poem—beginning, middle, and end, or before, during, and after.

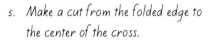

WORK YOUR LAZY HAND

With this technique you'll need pen and paper. If you prefer typing, try to put it aside for the moment. Any resistance you might feel indicates your brain is building new neurological pathways.

Do you usually write with your right hand? Here, you'll write and draw with your left. Are you left-handed? You'll use your right hand. Many people report that their "inner child" emerges with this exercise—the part of your personality that's more spontaneous and playful than the public "you."

Refer to the dialogue exercise in the previous chapter (Point of View, pp. 38-40). Now, write a few lines of dialogue using your non-dominant hand. Then, with your dominant hand, respond to those lines from your present-day or future self. When you've finished, compare the two and see if you notice a difference in voice.

Use this same method (it doesn't matter which hand is which) to write a dialogue between your most confident self and your inner critic—who may just be your biggest antagonist of all!

VILLAINOUS VOICES

In a story, the reader sides with the protagonist: the main character, the lead actor. It's the character we find ourselves rooting for. The antagonist, on the other hand, is often the one who causes problems: the villain, the one who creates the story's tension. They're the character we hope gets the short end of the stick. In this activity, the two change places!

Have you ever read *The True Story of the Three Little Pigs* by "A. Wolf"? (The author is actually Jon Scieszka.) As the title suggests, you don't usually hear the wolf's take on the classic folk tale. In *Wicked*, Gregory Maguire writes a back story for the *The Wonderful Wizard of Oz*, giving the villain— that is, the Wicked Witch of the West—the leading role; this is a complete departure from the original!

If you can, read *The True Story of the Three Little Pigs* before doing this activity. In case you can't (spoiler alert!), here are a few key points: Wolf had a terrible cold, and he was really just looking for a cup of sugar for his dear old granny's birthday cake. He couldn't help sneezing and swore he had no intention of causing any harm.

Now it's your turn. List a few people with whom you've had a disagreement. People you've argued with. People who see a situation from a different vantage point than you. Anyone in your life is fair game:

Your mother
Your father
A sibling
Other relative
A friend or ex-friend
A teacher
A pet

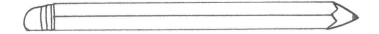

Think about the argument:

Where were you? (Scene)
What happened? (Action)
What was said? (Dialogue)

If it helps to take notes first, or jot down key points, go for it!

Now retell that story, only this time as the person you clashed with. Invite them to speak as the protagonist. Look for the positive thinking that you couldn't see in the heat of emotion. Be honest. What do you think motivated them—and now you?

Why would you want to do this? Writing-wise, it helps you get into the head of each of your characters to make them more complex, authentic, and honest. You want them to ring true, even if they're fictional.

In real life, this helps you empathize with others, improving your people skills. It gives you clarity of logic, helping you to better understand why people act or say what they do. You may discover that making assumptions about someone's behavior doesn't always give you the full truth of a situation.

CHAPTER

6

Trash to Treasure

BOOK BYTE WITH A MARBLEIZED COVER

How do you cope? Find a strategy that's uniquely yours. Create a hidden pocket to hold a personal moment of transformation.

Here you'll make a tiny book that transforms used tea bags into something beautiful.

Book Byte: Begin with a flyer, or any paper that's been used on one side before.
Directions:

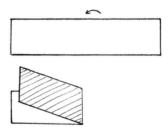

1. Cut the page into strips, lengthwise or width-wise. We've cut it into seven strips here.

2. Take one of the strips and fold it in half with the printed side out.

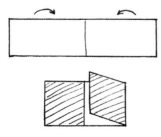

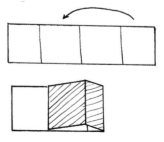

3. Fold both outer edges into the center.

4. Open the strip completely. Now fold the right edge in so it hits the first fold on the left.

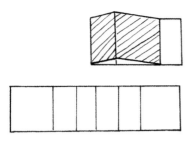

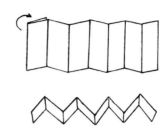

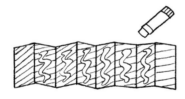

5. Open the strip again. Now fold the left edge in so it hits the first fold on the right. Now you should have five folds that delineate four small rectangles and two longer rectangles at the ends.

6. Next you'll make the strip into an "accordion." Do this by folding one of the long panels in half toward the back. Then continue to gather the panels together until all the panels are stacked. When you let go, you have four "mountains" and three "valleys."

7. Turn it over and apply glue to the middle six panels of your accordion, on the printed side. Gather it back together and press. You'll now have a blank, four-spread book.

8. You could collage with colored paper or images from magazines, or you could make something special to cover the book by using the following directions.

Marbleized Cover: Your book byte is now ready for your marbleized tea bag cover!

What you'll need:

- Small pan with sides (for your paint palette)
- Used, dried tea bags (you'll use only the paper)
- Scissors
- Shaving cream (plain, with no aloe or other emollients)
- Paint in several colors (watercolor is easiest to clean up)
- Pencil
- Newspaper or an old phone book or a towel (as surface protection)
- Spatula or a used plastic gift card
- Glue stick
- Spoon, or paintbrush if your paint is in jars

Optional:

- Glitter, or paint containing glitter

These directions are for a single book, but you'll want to make more than one piece of tea bag paper because of the effort involved—and how much you'll love your results!

Directions:

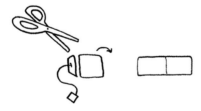 

1. Open the tea bag and shake the tea leaves into your compost bin or outside under a plant. Some tea bags will need you to cut off the staple that holds the string on. Others can be gently pulled apart.

2. To prepare your paint setup, cover the bottom of your pan with a thin layer of shaving cream.

3. Now apply dollops of paint to the shaving cream "canvas." If your paint is in bottles, squirt it on in squiggles; if in jars, use a spoon or fully-loaded paintbrush.

4. Using your pencil, swirl the paint minimally across the surface, once or twice. Avoid mixing — it will muddy your results.

 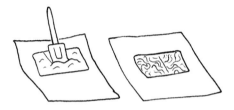

5. Lay your tea bag paper onto the painted shaving cream, pressing it into the paint so the entire paper meets the surface and picks up the design.

6. Pull the paper off, and put it shaving-cream-side up onto your newsprint. Use your spatula or plastic card to scrape off the excess shaving cream. If you're using glitter paint, you can apply it to the paper now, or after it's dry. When you're finished, move the paper onto another piece of newsprint to prevent sticking.

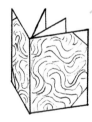

7. When it's dry, you're ready to apply your tea bag creation to your book byte. Just glue it to the first and last panels and trim off the excess. Or, if you prefer a collage-effect cover, rip your marbleized paper into pieces and glue them on.

Your book byte is ready to hold your proudest poem or other short piece. (See "Haiku Holder" in Chapter Four for short-form ideas.)

BLIND WRITING

This tool will keep you moving forward. Simply cover each line you finish writing with a piece of paper, so only the line you're working on is visible. Or, if you're on the computer, shrink your writing window so you can only see one line at a time.

The idea behind blocking out what's already written is that it keeps you from getting picky about your writing before the first draft is finished. This is an especially good strategy for perfectionists, who can get bogged down by self-criticism. It's a great way to beat a nagging internal editor.

Why would you want to wait to call in your inner editor? Your editor-self uses a different skill set that can stifle the wonderfully messy, exploratory,

Blogging 2.0

I started keeping a journal in first grade, but it took on new meaning with the advent of the Internet. Writing in a private, paper journal was the first step—for record-keeping, for copying, for planning, for dreaming—but keeping a blog came next. Sometimes it was rewriting my own journal entries to present a more refined and reserved form of expression that my friends could read, and other times it was a way to meet new people by throwing my thoughts, opinions, and questions out into the ether and letting people discover them. Then blogging went 2.0 and became a way for people to create a brand for themselves and to write more professionally, but still with a personal bent. It's more edited, but still a way for people to work out problems and discover themselves—in a pubic sphere, a meta-journal with comments and hyperlinks. That circular writing and publishing model is where I've met some of my best friends, acquired my greatest mentors, and discovered my role models. Writing separately but together has informed my most personal analog journaling. It's now what I respond to, what I incorporate into my own voice, and what informs the person I am becoming.

—Sarah Hannah Gomez, MA, MSLIS (personal communication, 2018)

and sometimes chaotic nature of first drafts. You can always pick up the mechanics later. With Blind Writing, you can let early drafts have their way. Let your writing go all over the place!

You can reign it in later if you decide you'd like to work more with these thoughts, themes, or ideas. But either way, know that whether you mine these pages or not, the process of writing *whatever*, without worry, is powerful for insight as well as for coping and problem solving.

Try it! Write for twenty minutes with just the line you're writing visible. Is your first draft freer? More spontaneous? Does it have more energy? Is your output more substantial? If so, good for you! Use the Blind Writing tool next time you get stuck. If not, good for you! You tried something new.

TRANSFORMING TROUBLES

We all have metaphorical trash in our lives. Bullies, disagreements, pain, failure, lack of confidence, betrayal, death. What's yours?

Some trash we can't do a thing about, but there are strategies out there to help us cope. Remembering those strategies is sometimes difficult when we're in the middle of our troubles. It's hard to be logical when we're emotional.

Here, you'll create another book, this one with an elegant cover made from old paper—a tangible metaphor for transforming trash into treasure. It will also remind you of your coping strategies and a personal moment of transformation.

For the inside pages, reread and follow the directions for the three-spread book in Chapter Five. If you use 8 ½ by 11" paper, the new book's pages will fit inside the handmade-paper cover. This one won't be reversible, but it will give you a secret compartment.

What you'll need:

- Colorful, used paper with a matte finish—old flyers, color printouts. It can be printed on both sides as long as there's at least one blank margin for you write on. This random paper will ultimately become your handmade-paper cover, so consider the colors you collect. (Avoid slick paper as its fibers are slippery and won't readily bind with themselves or other paper.)
- Embroidery hoop. Its diameter must be at least seven inches, and not much bigger, or your cover will dwarf your finished book. Hoops are available in thrift or craft stores; either wood or plastic will work.
- Watertight basin big enough to hold your embroidery hoop—and your fingers!
- Two pieces of plastic window screening, cut larger than the hoop.

- Blender
- Tabletop protector such as newspaper or a towel
- Water
- Sponge

Optional:
- Thin ribbon

Directions:

1. Begin by writing! On the margins and blank areas of your scrap paper, note those things that drive you crazy, memories that hurt, situations that make you angry, injustices, anxieties. Students have written about gossip, bullies, war, humiliation, divorce, the death of a friend or relative, money worries, sibling fights, rejection, loss of something cherished, sickness, depression, failing a class . . .

2. This step feels really good. Tear the paper into nickel-sized pieces. If you want to make certain colors, sort as you tear, putting your color choices into bowls.

3. Fill the blender with water (almost to the top) and throw in a handful of torn paper.

4. Blend on a medium speed. How long you leave the blender on will determine how many bits of letters and print are retained from the scraps. Bright and neon scraps will pop. Experiment! If you blend until you no longer see scraps, the colors will mix together almost like paint — for example, red and yellow scraps will make orange. If you stop sooner, solid bits will remain intact and give the final paper a fun confetti feel.

5. Pour the pulp into your basin and add more water until the mixture is more or less the consistency of egg-drop soup or a melty milkshake. You can add pulp or water at any time to get the consistency you want.

6. Place a piece of screen over the embroidery hoop. Secure it with the second section of hoop, as though it were a piece of material to be embroidered, and tighten, like the screen in a window.

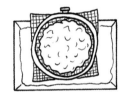

7. Dip the hoop into the basin and scoop up enough pulp so that a thin layer of it is left on the screen when you pull it up out of the water. Don't worry — if you don't like your results you can just toss the screen back into the water, swish it around, and dip it again. If the pulp is too thick, the dried paper will crack when folded. If it's too thin, the paper will tear and be more translucent. In either case, no big deal — you can use either "mistake" for collage.

8. Working over your tabletop protector, place another piece of screen over the pulp. You now have a pulp "sandwich": screen, pulp, screen.

9. Remove the embroidery hoop without disturbing your screen-and-pulp sandwich.

10. Now, press your slightly damp sponge onto the top screen to absorb some of the water. Squeeze the accumulated water back into the basin. (Papermakers call this "scooching.") Continue to pat (not wipe) the screened-in pulp until the sandwich is no longer dripping and the paper fibers are cohesive. The paper should hold together as you peel off the screens.

11. The way you dry your paper can affect its texture. Here are a few suggestions:

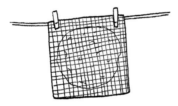

• Hang your pulp sandwich with both screens still attached. You'll end up with a fine grid texture on both sides.

• Remove both screens and lay the paper between newspaper. If it's still wet enough, your paper will have a wavy surface.

• Remove one screen and slap the paper onto a countertop or window. This will give the contacted side a slick finish.

For Some Cool Effects . . .

. . . take these additional steps. You'll need two extra screen pieces. Make your first piece of paper, press the excess water off with a sponge, then take off the top screen and set it aside. Using a new piece of screen, make a second piece of paper, press it with the sponge, and take off this top screen as well. On one of the two pieces of paper, draw a design in coarse sand as though you were a Dine or Buddhist sandpainter. Put the other paper on top so that the sand is the inside of the paper sandwich. Sponge the screen again. Your design will appear in relief when the paper dries. Or use an actual ribbon (instead of a ribbon of sand), draping it in a straight line across the middle of one circle of paper. Apply the second circle to the first — you'll again have a screen sandwich, but with two pieces of paper with a ribbon inside. Sponge again — the pressure will help fuse the two papers. The point of the ribbon is to be able to tie your half-circle cover (which should resemble a taco) shut with a bow once it's dry, so make sure your ribbon tails are long enough.

When your fabulous cover is dry, fold it in half. Now it's time to get started on a book that's worthy of this masterpiece!

Finish making the three-spread blank book, if you haven't already. Mark an X on the front and back panel—these will be glued onto your handmade cover once it's dry. The other pages are for recording your trash-to-treasure strategies.

Now it's time to write! You could start with a title on the first page of the book: "Transformational Strategies" or "Trash to Treasure."

Gather ideas that you, your friends, or your family have successfully used to transform a bad situation into a tolerable one—or even an ultimate victory. Don't feel like you have to fill the pages right now. You can have your antennae up and add to it over time. But you no doubt know some strategies already. If not, consider these:

Talk through a situation with a friend.
Listen to uplifting music.

Write in your journal.

Take a walk, a run, a hike, or a bike trip.

Hit a baseball. Kick a soccer ball.

Watch a movie.

Delve into a book that takes you away—or a book that makes you look the situation in the face.

Take some time to enjoy nature.

Now let's open up a secret space in this book to write about a transformation—a moment when you successfully turned a situation around.

Open your small book all the way back to its 8½ by 11" size. Now, write about that time you made a bad situation better. Or the time when something in your life stank and your attitude made it smell sweet. Then refold the little book and glue the X-marked pages into your dried handmade paper cover.

The next time something trashy happens, this small book will remind you of strategies you can use and a moment when you've triumphed before. If you did it once, you can do it again!

Remember that optional ribbon? Use it to tie your creation with a bow—a gift to yourself.

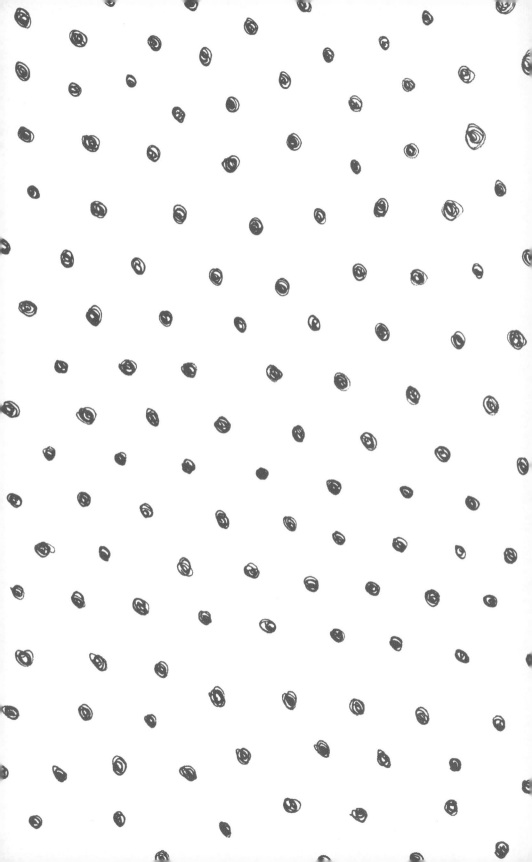

CHAPTER

7

Follow Your Dreams

RAPID WRITING

Got dreams? Daydreams, nightmares?
Use them to power up your journey.

Rapid writing draws on your subconscious mind, where your creativity is most active. It's sometimes called hot penning, speed writing, freewriting, or stream of consciousness. Using this technique, you can write with either pen and paper or the keyboard—but realize that your choice of medium will make a difference. Recent studies have found a correlation between hand writing and a higher number of ideas generated. We've found that pen and paper will produce a more personal page and offer visual hints of who you are. Some writers say the content will be more expressive, too. Even today, many authors write their first draft by hand. Other people swear by the keyboard. So, feel free to write either way.

If you've never tried rapid writing, start a timer for five minutes and make a commitment to keep your pen moving across the page. Don't stop. If you get stuck, just repeating a word or drawing a circle or making an up-and-down motion with your pen keeps the circuit between your hand and the language center in your brain open. You can also invent your own default phrase or mantra—keep writing the phrase "what else," "what next," or "forward" until the next thought or idea arrives. The flow of words doesn't have to make sense. It can jump around from one topic to another—or not.

Why would you want to do this? Pushing yourself with a pen lets you pull out that power of what's just under the surface. It makes connections in your mind. Get ready to be surprised!

Many authors have extolled the value of this kind of writing. Brenda Ueland, in *If You Want To Write*, talks about this creative work as being "like a faucet: nothing comes unless you turn it on, and the more you turn it on, the more comes out." In *The Artist's Way*, Julia Cameron suggests writing three pages every morning when you get up. Marge sets a timer to write for 23 minutes.

Try rapid writing in silence. Try it with music on, or haul yourself outside to rapid write in nature.

If you're true to this practice over time, you might find you're more productive and creative. You might feel like you're using more complex thinking—that you've attained more clarity on who you are.

DREAMS GET REAL

Writing down your dreams gives you power. Dreams develop your awareness, and writing them down sparks magic. Consider making a commitment to record your dreams as a gift to yourself.

You can harness that power and magic by documenting either your night dreams, which come from your subconscious, or your daydreams, which involve more of your consciousness and will. Committing your dreams to paper can give them substance and even a sense of reality, if that's what you're after.

Night Dreams

Some people keep a notebook next to their bed to capture their dreams—the dreams that wake them up or the ones they remember first thing in the morning.

Do you have a recurring night dream? Or a dream so vivid that it gets stuck in your head? Write it down. Try to catch your night (or nap!) dreams as soon as you wake up, before they fade.

Let the meaning of your night dream bubble up into your awareness, like Maria did in the example below. Give yourself permission to accept it as a kind of illustration that doesn't need to be completely understood.

Night Dreams as a Diagnostic Tool

Maria wrote down her dreams for a year. All her dreams were about flying and crashing: in a hot air balloon, a jet, a helicopter, even without an aircraft, just flapping her arms and falling to earth. Maria eventually interpreted her dreams to be a metaphor for her up and down moods. Shortly afterward, discussing this interpretation helped her medical professionals to diagnose her as bipolar. As a result, she received medication that allowed her to live a normal, even extraordinary life.

Daydreams

What are the things you want to happen in your life? When you spend time thinking about them, you're daydreaming. Having that daydream is like finding a seed. Writing it down is like planting it. So write it down! Even better, write down more than one so you have a few to choose from.

Daydream Believer

This one's about me, Marge. In my middle school English class, we were all asked to write our autobiographies. We were supposed to include a section about our imagined futures—what we were dreaming for ourselves. I dreamed of myself as a writer and teacher. In college, though, I majored in psychology and used that degree in my early career as a human-relations trainer. But later, leaving that job because of a move, I was able to follow my passion and started to sell my writing. I had forgotten all about what I had dreamed in middle school until many years later, when my parents sent me a box of my school memorabilia. I realized I had become exactly what I wrote about in my daydream.

Think about what you want to invite into your life—you can't control your night dreams, but you can control your daydreams!

You can write down your dreams in your journal, or, perhaps for your favorites, use the pop-up book format that follows.

POP-UP BOOK

Here, you'll be making a two-sided pop-up book. Choose one of your night dreams and one of your daydreams and think of an image to represent each.

In planning each pop-up, keep in mind you can write on the pop-up part of the page, or on any blank space left after the pop-up image has popped!

Now you're ready to create the physical book.

Directions:

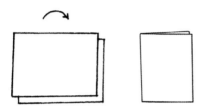

1. Place one piece of paper on top of another piece that's the same size (but not necessarily the same color!). Now fold them in half together, either crosswise or lengthwise (hamburger or hot dog fold).

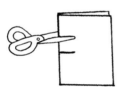

2. Cut a pair of slits from the folded edge some distance (half an inch to two inches) into the panel. You'll be cutting through four layers.

   Be sure to leave a margin — don't cut all the way through to the edge. The slits should be of equal length and can be cut into the middle of the fold or off center.

   How far apart from each other should the slits should be? You decide. Your choice will determine how much uninterrupted writing and art space you'll have to work with and how big a platform you'll need for your glued-on element. You might even need two pedestals if your pop-up image is long and skinny. (If this isn't clear yet, keep reading.)

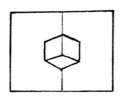 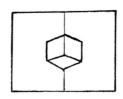

3. Now separate the pages. Push out the tabs created by the slits, refolding the tabs in the opposite direction. Doing this will define a cubic or rectangular space.

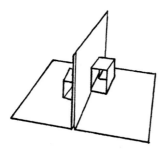

4. Place the pages on the table so they form L shapes with one L facing backwards. Now glue the facing panels together, leaving the cubes sticking out. (Avoid getting glue on them.) You should be looking at an upside-down T, with a cube on each side of the vertical panel.

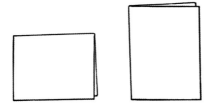

5. Now, close it. The fold of the book could be at the top, like a wall calendar, or the fold could be on the left, like a standard book.

   Your double-sided dream book is now ready for your images and words describing one of your daydreams and one of your night dreams.

6. Create your image. The paper for your image could be of any contrasting color, texture, or thickness. You could paint, draw, or even collage your image onto the paper using scraps. But the size of your artwork will be limited. If your image is big, when you close your book, it may hang out like a tongue. Unless you want that effect, paper-clip your image to the front of the pedestal and close the book to see if the size works for your idea.

7. Ready to write? Feel free to play with the format and genre. For example:

    - Write your dream as a poem.
    - Tell the story as flash fiction (a very short story).
    - Report your dream as though it was a news story.
    - Write it in any of the other forms or formats found in this book, such as an "I Remember" poem (Chapter Two) or from different points of view (Chapter Four).

Cameron, J. (2002). *The artist's way*. New York, NY: TarcherPerigee. (Original work published 1992)

Ueland, B. (2002). *If you want to write: A book about art, independence and spirit*. Minneapolis, MN: Graywolf Press.

CHAPTER

8

The Art of the Unexpected

CLUSTERING

*Start small and specific; end up
with something big and unexpected.*

Clustering is a kind of brainstorming that can enrich your thinking and provide new topics and approaches to your pages. This linguistic tool, which works with spatial thinking, lights up the creative parts of your brain. Gabriele Lusser Rico talks about this in her book, *Writing the Natural Way: Using Right-Brain Techniques to Release Your Expressive Powers.* You might have used a technique like this in school to document what you know about a topic, or to see the relationship between threads for an essay—but with this approach to clustering, anything goes!

First, write a word in the middle of the page. You could choose a word from one of your lists or a word plucked from your environment, say, the word "blue." Now, circle it. Using lines leading out from that circle, begin to cluster thoughts, words, and ideas that the first word suggests. Each word may begin a cluster of its own. With each different idea, draw a new line. Let your words and ideas flow! Sometimes two concepts generated separately can be connected, like "storm" and "eye of the hurricane" in our example (opposite page). Most people are surprised and entertained by how far clustering takes them.

Clustering can lead you to the unexpected. When the writer of this example saw the word "nervous" hit the page, she knew she wanted to write about the time she performed in front of an audience and lost her place in the music.

As you're clustering, be ready for the moment when something clicks and you discover what you want to write about. When that happens, it's time to abandon your brainstorming and write the story or scene that the clustering brought you to.

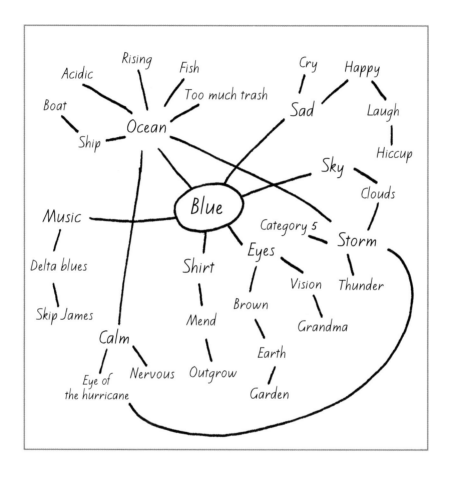

THREE WORDS △ △ △

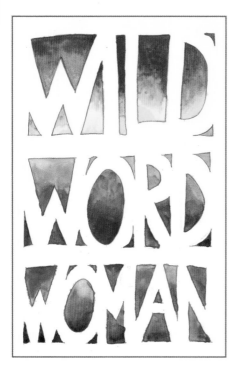

Start this fun draw-and-doodle project by claiming three words that describe you best. Okay, but why three words, not two, or four, or six?

The preference for threes is cultural. Many cultures and religions have a strong affinity for the number three. You may belong to a folktale tradition that includes stories of threes: "Three Little Pigs," "The Three Musketeers," "Three Blind Mice," or "The Three Billy Goats Gruff." Within some tales, three is the number of wishes granted or the number of challenges a hero must undertake.

The Rule of Thirds

Threes may also be important visually. Marianna Pegno, an innovative arts educator, says, "In the visual arts, compositions are stronger when there is an imbalance, since it keeps your eye moving throughout the entire work. If there is complete symmetry, the eye can get stuck bouncing between two points rather than exploring the entire artwork. The same goes for page layouts and graphic design. It's known as the rule of thirds." (M. Pegno, personal communication, 2018).

In other cultures—maybe yours!—different numbers are favored. For example, in many Native American artworks and folktales, four is prominent. There are four sacred mountains, four colors, four cardinal directions, and four stages of life.

Once you've come up with your three—or four, or five—personal words, write them on a piece of paper in some special way: in bubble script, calligraphy, ornamented letters, a fancy cursive, or different colors using paint, pencils, crayons, or markers. Fill the space around or within these words by doodling, cross hatching, painting, or pasting in photos or pictures from magazines. (For powerful inspiration on doodling, look up Zentangle online.)

The idea is to spend time with your selected words. As you work, let the meaning of the words—words that suggest your identity—settle into your mind. *Be* the one who is "Genuine, Optimistic, Intriguing," a "Savvy Geek Musician," "Artistic, Rebel, Wise," or "Smart, Pensive, Observant."

Consider hanging your finished word-inspired art by your workspace or in your room. Try doing another one after some time has passed to see what you can learn about yourself over time. You could give yourself a three- or four-word gift for your birthday each year!

You could even ask your favorite fictional characters to choose their own special words. Be present with those words. Think like the character while you color or doodle or paint. How do those attributes or descriptive words play out in the story or poem? If you try this with your own fictional characters, the experience can inform your subsequent writing. By flipping the switch on your visual artist, you'll push the word work forward in deeper ways.

You're the boss of how you use this activity. But understand that when you honor your characters' words with this tool, you'll be developing their all-important voices.

You can also push a story's emotional arcs by doing this exercise before and after a character's transformational moment. What does she leave behind? What does he strive for? Where are they headed (even if they don't know it yet)?

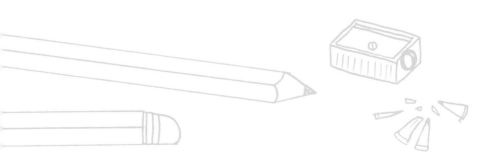

ALTERED BOOKS

Take a discarded book, and make some magic! Altered books use a traditional physical book as a medium for writing and art. What's so great about altered books? You get to play creatively while exercising your word, logic, art, and kinesthetic skills.

Today, these ways of working are often bypassed by technology. Technology rocks, but, because so much of it is automated, it can also take away from a depth of experience. Instead of twisting a lens, we press a button. Instead of whittling our pencil with a knife, or even grinding it in a manual sharpener, we stick it into a machine. Instead of bending down to plant a seed or climbing a ladder to harvest a fruit, we buy our food at the store.

By altering books, you do something physical. In this activity, a book headed for the landfill becomes a medium for two and three-dimensional art, a place to "find" poems, or a beautiful work of art to show off mementos and preserve your writing.

Look for books to alter in thrift stores, yard sales, or at library discard events. Three broad approaches to altering books include:

1. Working with the outside of the book. See examples (A), a "wrap," and (B), "grass" pulled from a paperback.
2. Creating structure. This includes folding (C), carving (D), and niche-creating (E).
3. Working with the pages. Alter them by tearing (F), cutting (G), or collaging (H). You might use your book's existing theme to inspire you to write about that theme and interact with it. For example, if your book is about trains, it will likely have photos of trains just begging for you to glue in tangible objects illustrating your train stories in the form of tickets, schedules, trip photos, or the penny you squished on the tracks. You could even use gesso on some of the pages to white them out (I) and provide blank areas for your writing and art.

1. A. B.

2. C. D.

E.

With altered books, experimentation is key. You may want to start with a "sampler" book—trying different techniques on each page to find a concept you want to explore. Use the examples above and what you find on the Internet for inspiration. There are lots of websites for altered books, many showing exquisite works of art.

And now, here's where the writing comes in.

Use some of the tools and writing prompts you've already read about in this book. For example, use negative space (Chapter Three, Found Poems, or the window technique from Chapter Nine, or see example J at right). Let an image inspire you to write from its viewpoint on a gesso-ed or collaged page (Chapter Four, Point of View).

You could also retain some of the content on existing pages of your reclaimed book. For example, write about yourself under the About the

3.

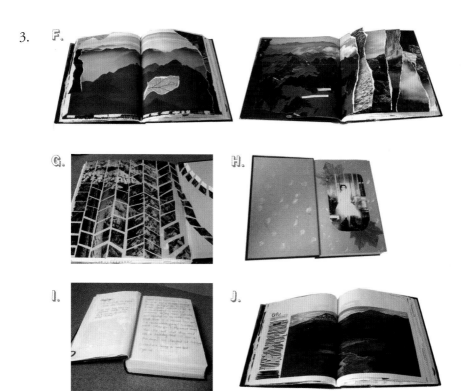

Author heading, or replace the titles on the Table of Contents page with the chapters of your life. Other techniques you might find useful:

- Hide writing or images under flaps
- Cut and curl
- Sew
- Bead
- Glue pages together
- Paint over your pages, as a character in Marcus Zusak's *The Book Thief* does
- Tear edges (the direction of your tear determines whether you have a white edge or not)

But don't stop there! You can also:

- Cut strips of paper for grass or hair
- Incorporate origami
- Make drawers
- Weave
- Stencil
- Wad up small pieces of paper to make pebbles or shape larger ones for stone
- Create three-dimensional scenes, as in *The Fairy-Tale Princess: Seven Classic Stories from the Enchanted Forest* by Su Blackwell and Wendy Jones

Here's the bottom line: Anything you can do with a piece of paper, you can do with an altered book!

Rico, G. L. (2000). *Writing the natural way: Turn the task of writing into the joy of writing.* New York, NY: TarcherPerigee. (Original work published 1983)

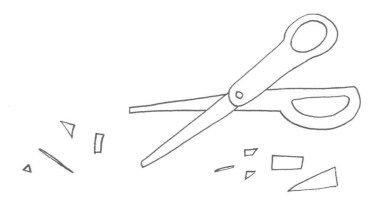

CHAPTER
9

*Talk
Back*

INTERLINEAR POETRY

Here's where it's okay to say exactly what you think!

Interlinear poetry is simply talking back to a poem line by line. If you're doing this by hand, write out a published poem in pencil, leaving space between lines. Respond to each line in pen, then erase the original lines.

To give this technique a try, let's consider Juanita Havill's "Alone Together."

Alone Together
I close my eyes
    feel the wind in my face.
    The hooves of my galloping horse
    pound to the speed of my heartbeats.
I lean forward
    and whisper in his ear:
    "We're raising dust in the field,
    alone together, you and I,
    and the sky belongs to us."
— Juanita Havill
(reprinted with permission of the author)

Now talk back to each line:

Alone Together
I know how it feels.
I close my eyes
You need to trust—
    feel the wind in my face.
    a strong wind can blow you over.
    The hooves of my galloping horse
    Jump clear!
    pound to the speed of my heartbeats.
    Synchronize your heart and your life.

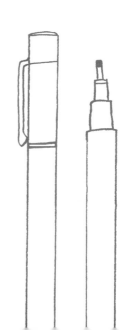

I lean forward

Don't lean too far, you'll fall into your oatmeal.

    and whisper in his ear:

    No one keeps secrets any more.

    "We're raising dust in the field,

    So watch out for those dust devils.

    alone together, you and I,

    Don't retreat into your head, alone.

    and the sky belongs to us."

You might not see the sky.

Now, delete Juanita's lines and see how your backtalk holds up all by itself. Let your backtalk stand as it is (as seen below) or use it as a first draft that you can edit at will.

I Know How It Feels

(After Juanita Havill's poem, "Alone Together")

I know how it feels.
You need to trust—
a strong wind can blow you over.
Jump clear!
Synchronize your heart and your life.
Don't lean too far, you'll fall into your oatmeal.
No one keeps secrets any more,
so watch out for those dust devils.
Don't retreat into your head, alone.
You might not see the sky.

REVIEWING AND PERSUADING ⁄ɯɯ⁄

Talking back helps you organize your thinking. However you choose to share your opinion—in the form of a review or to persuade—here are some ideas to talk back in a way that will help people listen.

1. First choose something you want to respond to—an event, situation, or something you saw. Something you care about.

2. Next, ask yourself why you feel the way you do. Jot down some notes. You may want to use the clustering tool in Chapter Eight or rapid writing tool in Chapter Seven.

3. Now let's organize that mess! There's a simple but essential formula for writing a persuasive piece:

   • Make your point.
   • List and explain the examples that prove your point.
   • Restate your point from the more fully explored perspective the reader now has.

As you write, you might also want to anticipate any objections your reader may have and address each one. This is like disarming your opponent. You show your readers that you have already considered their arguments, looked at the situation from their perspective, and still maintained your point of view. Here's an example of addressing anticipated points of view. (Two sentences do this overtly; can you spot them?)

Some people think they need to buy a car as soon as they're old enough. But even if you're old enough to have a car, you might not want one!

For one thing, they're expensive. Even a new car has maintenance costs and license fees, and an old one can break the bank with repairs. Any list of expenses also has to include gas, insurance, parking, oil changes, and car washes.

Health costs are an issue, too. Cars force you to sit a lot. Instead, you could be bicycling or walking or skateboarding and getting the exercise your body needs. Don't have the time to walk or bike? Subtract the time it takes to drive to the health club and all that unproductive movement, and maybe you do have time to walk, bike, or skate.

Having to drive somewhere quickly makes you feel different about your day. Because cars are fast, car culture can make you feel rushed. Walking and biking can slow down the perceived pace of your life. Instead of a landscape that rushes past your car window, you get to see details— the birds and flowers and the neighbor's new dog. As a pedestrian, you might be the first to notice changes in the area, like that new cafe.

Both your body and mind can tense up with the attention necessary to drive safely. Walking, biking, and taking public transportation can make you feel lighter. The weight of responsibility for your life and the lives of others is lifted. Walking and taking public transportation frees you to go into your creative mind and feed and enrich yourself. Some people who choose not to drive find that they're just plain happier.

And these are just the personal issues. There are planetary issues, too. Imagine if the world were free of greenhouse gasses from automobile emissions. Your friends with asthma wouldn't suffer or lag behind. Parks would replace huge piles of stinking, burning tires. Precious lives would not be tragically lost in accidents. Some wars over resources wouldn't be fought. Skies would not be choked with yellow smog.

As you can see, there are plenty of reasons to ditch car ownership. Not everyone can, but because of the many personal and global benefits, you might want to consider whether going car-free would make your life more carefree.

Now let's consider the opinion piece, where you express your views on a personal or political issue. Talk back to an unspoken rule, a person in power, or your community as a whole.

What do you want to change? Does it bother you when your library doesn't have the book or movie or music you want? Is there an injustice in your town, country, or the world that drives you crazy? Do you wish people in your community would be more respectful of teens? Have you noticed something crazy-wonderful that you admire and want to draw attention to?

By writing persuasively, you can make your readers think, or even inspire them to act. And your own burden might be lightened if you share it.

The first step in writing persuasively is to think the problem through and ask yourself: What's your idea? Who's your agent of change? The mayor or your city council might be able to help you add a bus route. The library has an acquisitions person who decides what books, movies, and music will be purchased. You could challenge your community to think about teens as people with feelings and positive attributes rather than judge them all by the destructive tendencies of a few.

The second step is to find out how to contact these agents of change. The mayor and city council could be a phone call away. In this case, your creative writing takes the form of notes or a script that you write in preparation for your conversation with that person. Your writing might take the form of an email—for example, if you want to contact the librarian who orders books and music for your library. To reach more than one agent of change in your community or world, consider reaching out to an audience through media such as the following:

Newspapers and magazines (school and community)
Bulletin boards
Local television and radio
Social media
Organizations with newsletters

Sometimes you'll want to write more than one type of persuasive piece. For example, you'll write a script for the conversation with the mayor and an essay for a larger audience who can be urged to contact that change agent as well.

One way to talk back persuasively is in a letter. *Bones of Faerie* fantasy writer Janni Lee Simner was a kid when McDonald's used to publish a calendar. They noted Christian and secular holidays—even some as minor as Groundhog Day—but not the High Holy Days she celebrated, such as Rosh Hashanah and Yom Kippur. Janni felt excluded. She wrote to them, and they responded with a letter of apology and some coupons. From then on, for as long as they published the calendar, they included the Jewish high holidays. "This was significant," Janni said, "because I realized I could speak up and people would listen. I found out it matters when something bothers me, and it's worth saying so."

Be careful with your actions. Some issues are emotional. They could result in a response that would be hostile or even unsafe. If you suspect your writing or actions may fall into this category, talk it over with a teacher or some other adult you trust.

When not responding is the better course of action, a journal entry might be the way to go. Sometimes it's enough to put your backtalk on the page, to just let it out. Studies have shown that putting negative thoughts into words on a page has physiological benefits. To honor the significance and transformation from something held inside to something on the page, rip it up and recycle it. (See Chapter Six.)

There's also the arts review, in which you talk back to someone else's creative work. Do you have a strong opinion on a book you've read? Have you recently discovered a song you love? Or seen a movie or read an article that made you angry? Have you read something wonderful that had a flaw you're itching to set right? Write an arts review!

First, read some online reviews so you're familiar with the form. Choose any piece of writing, music, dance, film, theater, or even a restaurant. Remember that angry or disrespectful reviews are often not read and don't have the impact that a more considered piece might have. You want to sound professional and fair. Balance your piece by noting at least one positive point. Even a review with mostly negative comments might begin with positives.

Here's a sample review of "I'm Nobody! Who are you?"

> Emily Dickinson's poem, "I'm Nobody! Who are you?" is justifiably admired. Her rhyme and rhythm are pleasing to the ear. She skillfully pulls in the reader by addressing them in second person ("Are you a nobody, too?"), almost as though she's putting her arm around the reader and saying, "we belong together."
>
> But, in my opinion, the poem's message has to be balanced. Certainly, hearing someone so admired and famous say she's a "nobody" can be comforting. But if you read the poem out loud, you're saying "I'm nobody" about yourself. It's a negative affirmation. Would you put that on your mirror? "I'm Nobody"? It's not what a psychologist would tell you to do today. As a poem it works, but as an approach to life, a blend of the two ideas might be more helpful: Everybody really is a nobody, but it's good to hold onto a belief in yourself as somebody.
>
> — KS and MP

You could send your review to an appropriate website for publication—perhaps the site where the original work appeared, or a newspaper, or your own blog, or other appropriate social media sites. Your opinion can matter to the artist you're reviewing, as well as to others who have experienced the work. You may even introduce others to the work. You don't have to be eighteen to "vote" on someone else's work!

Group Project: The Cash Mob

What are some ways you might act or use your writing to enlist the help of others to make a difference close to home?

For a course in Literary Citizenship, students in Oswego, New York planned a "cash mob" at a local independent bookstore. They recruited classmates, friends, faculty, family and community members to visit the bookstore during one predetermined 2-hour period. The objectives: spend a little money, meet new people, and draw attention to a valued town business.

The event was a win-win-win-win. The students coordinated and publicized (via social media and flyers) a major, successful public event. The bookstore sold plenty of books, magazines, postcards, and other merchandise. Authors reached more readers. And community ties were strengthened. In other words, it was successful and a lot of fun.

Where we spend our money—even if it's just a few dollars—can be a political statement. Purchasing books online through major retailers is convenient, but may contribute to putting small, local stores out of business. It's a complex issue, but in educating yourself you may find that supporting independent bookstores aligns with your values as a reader and/or writer.

— Donna Steiner, award-winning nonfiction writer and poet (personal communication, 2018)

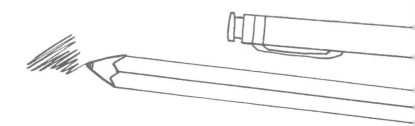

WINDOWS

If all this backtalk has you feeling a bit contrarian, here's a technique that could shift you into the positive.

Choose a line that holds its opposite within it. For example:

> Words hold us back.
> Words can crush what holds us back.

What you'll need:

- Blank piece of paper any size
- Box cutter or utility knife
- Pencil
- Old phone book or cutting board
- Marker
- Lamp or sunny window

Directions:

1. Choose a line or two from this chapter, or any of your writing, or any line written by anybody that you'd like to talk back to. Here are more examples if you get stuck:

> Everything changes.
> Everything but our friendship changes.

> I learned a lot.
> I learned that I have a lot to learn.

> You have everything.
> If you have your health, you have everything.

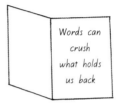

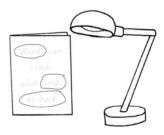

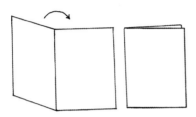

A good idea.

It seemed like a good idea at the time.

Everybody knows.

Everybody who's met you knows you rock!

2. Fold your paper in half, then open it back up.

3. Write the longer sentence you chose on the right-hand panel, large enough to use the whole space (but not too close to the edge). For example: "Words can crush what holds us back."

Words can
crush
what holds
us back

Words
hold
us back

4. Decide which words within the line you chose could create their own phrase or sentence. "Words hold us back." (It's this phrase, the extracted sequence, that will be seen first.)

5. Refold the paper and hold it up to the lamp or window. Circle each of the words you've extracted.

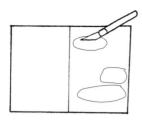 

6. Unfold and cut windows around those circles, using the utility knife against the cutting board or old phone book.

7. Refold and be amazed!

You can use this cool technique to find oppositions within your writing or to play with creating sentences that could shift in meaning.

Dickinson, E. (1924). *Complete poems*. New York, NY: Little, Brown, and Company.

Havill, J. (2017). *Alone together*. In M. H. Barnes, *The Best of Today's Little Ditty 2016*. Igloo Island Press.

CHAPTER

10

Heroes

PERSONALIZED STATIONERY

Tap into your inner wisdom; seek wisdom figures.

Emailing and texting are easy—in some ways even too easy. Snail-mail isn't used as much as it used to be. Siraaj, a university student, told us his last handwritten letter was to Santa Claus! But maybe that's a reason you should use it. Anthony Matthews, the man behind the famous website, "Dear Customer Relations," writes his complaint letters on paper and mails them because he believes they're more likely to be read in that form than if they were emailed. His letters are often funny, sarcastic, and ironic—and they usually get results.

The written word may last longer on paper than in digital form. Some scholars are even concerned that future historians will lack the kind of details that were once preserved in personal letters, diaries, and business correspondence. Before paper, we pressed our records, messages, and stories into clay, scratched them into bones, and carved them into stone. It seems our words are becoming more and more ephemeral!

Even today most people like having something tangible to hold onto. They enjoy finding a "present" in their mailbox, something they can read without being plugged in.

Chapter Seven talks about the differences between writing by hand and typing. Another point: digital devices allow one to obsessively edit. Editing is necessary, but over-edited pieces sometimes lose their punch. On paper, you put down what first comes to mind, so your language is fresher. Paper still allows more than one draft, but you're less likely to waste time making insignificant changes. Author Meg Files (*Writing What You Know*) claims she can tell the difference between a handwritten and a typed first draft!

Personalized stationery makes letters fun to write and receive. The art can be businesslike or flowery, a professional logo or a doodle. Your recipient or audience will suggest what kind of design you'll use. You may be writing to an official or someone you know well, perhaps someone you care about deeply. Some people are only reachable by letter—for example, people who don't have access to computers, or those who choose not to use them for a variety of reasons. Sometimes you'll only have a physical address.

Personalized stationery is another way to honor your writing. It could be a one-of-a-kind work of art on which you'll write thoughts to your new romantic interest, or an often-copied original letterhead that represents the public "you." You could even have a favorite quote or a personal motto.

Roger Sather, a writer who unfortunately couldn't spell, embraced his challenge with humor on his personal stationery. At the top it said, "I have no respect for people who only have one way to spell a word."

Here are some ideas for your stationery:

- Make a stamp! This allows you to make multiple copies without using a copy machine or computer or printer. Carve a design into a suitable material. You can buy foam board or a gum eraser especially designed for carving. You can even use the flat side of a potato half! For all of these, use an ink pad or spread a thin layer of paint on a plate or jar cover, dip your carving into the paint or ink, and stamp it on your paper.
- Alter the page with a crazy hole puncher or specialty-edged scissors.
- Use one of the techniques described elsewhere in the book, such as collage, paint, doodles, or handmade paper.
- Create a design on your computer and print it out on your favorite paper.

LETTERS

Letters can be a vehicle to work through issues. In *The Diary of a Young Girl*, Anne Frank writes a series of letters to Kitty, an imaginary friend. Writing as though she were talking to a specific person helped her focus her thoughts and, some say, endure her circumstances living secretly in an attic with a cast of difficult characters. Other books have also followed this format to share nonfiction, such as *Diary of Latoya Hunter* by Latoya Hunter, or *Zlata's Diary: A Child's Life in Sarajevo* by Zlata Filipovic. Some writers are successful in using letters to tell a fictional tale, like Beverly Cleary's *Dear Mr. Henshaw*, or Bram Stoker's *Dracula*.

One of the most personally helpful kinds of letter you can write is a letter of gratitude. Research shows that remembering a kindness or a special connection that you are grateful for will benefit your emotional wellbeing. People who habitually express gratitude are happier! Talk show host Jimmy Fallon has turned the idea of thank-you notes (real or imagined) into a platform for comedy. He knows he can count on his audience's familiarity with the form to recognize when it has gone wrong—and laugh!

Think about how you felt when someone took the time to thank you. Gratitude letters can make people feel validated, appreciated, and valued. Your words could make someone's day.

Write a letter using your personalized stationery or create a pop-up card (see Chapter Seven). Be specific in your letter—remember, details rule! The more specific the praise, the better. Your gratitude letter can be long or short. If you feel stuck, try using the format: When you _____, I felt _____.

Now, send it off and enjoy the good feelings.

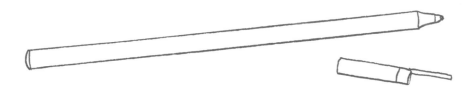

BRINGING OUT YOUR INNER WISDOM

Hero letters are powerful, so take a deep breath and get ready! Many find new nuggets of personal wisdom through this activity. This process will encourage you to think about positive traits. You'll see your challenges through different eyes. You'll become aware of things you want to change, or things you didn't know could be changed. You might just discover resources you already have, abilities that you can put to work right away.

What do heroes do? Heroes can be crucial to our dreams and decisions. They're our models and examples. They may even offer us a road map and specific ideas for setting our own goals and realizing our dreams. The aim of *The Seven Spiritual Laws of Superheroes* (written jointly by Dr. Deepak Chopra and his son Gotham) is to present ways you can use these heroes to help transform your life.

People can have a positive influence on us even if they're not in our lives directly. They don't even need to be alive—they don't even need to be people—for us to learn from them.

Fold a piece of paper into thirds, lengthwise, so you have three long panels.

On the first panel, list people you believe are heroes. Remember, the hero could be living or dead, real or fictitious. It could even be your cat! If you have a hard time with this, skip to the middle panel.

In the middle panel, list traits that you believe make a person a hero or a wisdom figure. (If this brings some heroes to mind, go back and add those names to the first panel.) Are they honest? Good? Caring? Would you say they're hard workers? Big-hearted? Do they break ground? Are they pioneers? Smart? What ways might a hero express these qualities? Would a hero always fight for what's right? How far would a hero go to help someone else? Would a hero be modest, doing good deeds behind the scenes? Let the lists feed each other. If you think, for example, Frida Kahlo or Thomas Edison belongs on the list of heroes, what particular quality or attribute would qualify them?

You can also approach this portion of the activity through categories. Try pulling your heroes from the following list:

artists	religious figures
sports figures	family and friends
inventors	comics
those who faced great obstacles	movie characters/directors/actors
community leaders	musicians
helping professionals	writers
fire fighters	human rights advocates
medical workers	teachers
scientists	rescuers

On the third panel, list some problems or challenges you're facing right now. Maybe there's a part of your life that you wish was smoother. Do you have a personal relationship that needs fixing? Or something you want to accomplish? Maybe you're faced with a puzzle you haven't quite figured out.

Others have listed problems or challenges related to relationships, safety, rules, improving a skill, loss, military deployment, self-esteem, resources, work or school, health, or community.

Now review your attribute, hero, and challenge lists. Choose a hero and an attribute or two that best represents them. Write them a letter. Though your challenge might be a serious one, you're allowed to be funny! Each letter should include:

1. At least one attribute you admire in the hero.
2. An explanation of one problem or challenge you're facing.
3. A request for advice.

Here are three examples of a hero letter:

Dear Frida Kahlo,

   You are my hero. I look up to you because you are a creative person. I want to be just like you, a magnificent painter with great qualities.

   I need someone to talk to about my brother and sister. Do you have any advice on how to get along with them when they act really annoying?

   And, while I'm at it, how did you learn to paint so well?

Love,
Vee. G

Dear Mr. Menaugh,

   I admire you because you make learning fun and you make your students see things from another perspective.

   I need help in becoming more responsible. Can you give me some advice?

Sincerely,
Juan L.

P.S. You're an awesome teacher. Keep up the excellent work.

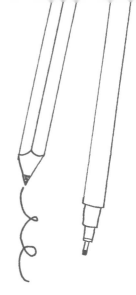

Dear Amy,

I miss you so much. You cared about me like I was your real family.

I want to be like you. What do I need to do to be a good leader and an inspiring person?

Can you give me some advice?

Love,
Vicky H.

Let these examples inspire you to write your own letter. You may want to write an even longer letter, explaining your challenge in more detail.

Close your eyes and imagine the hero to whom you wrote. Think of the specific reason, the attributes that caused you to choose your hero. Was it their kindness, their humility, their energy, their commitment to a cause, or something else?

Take a deep breath. Hold it, then let it out slowly. Do this three times, imagining you are the hero. Recognize that if you valued a certain attribute—say, generosity—you yourself have the seed of that same trait in you. Accept that you have that budding quality. "Wear" your hero's attribute.

Now, as that hero, with that attribute, answer the letter you received. Here are the responses to the previous examples:

Dear Vee,

Thank you for saying you admire my art! It's wonderful to know that you look up to me. Maybe someday you will be in my position and be creating amazing paintings that will be in museums all over the world.

Here's my advice on painting: Practice really does make perfect!

And about your brother and sister: It may seem like they will always bug you! But they won't. Try hard to be nice to them. Some day they will grow up and you will be friends for life.

Love,
Frida Kahlo

P.S. Don't forget to practice! Practice! Practice!
P.S.S. Invite me to your first art show!

Dear Juan,

Thank you for seeing me as your hero. I really appreciate it. In your letter, you said you needed help on becoming more responsible. Don't worry; you are not alone. There are many others who would like to become more responsible. The first step is to become organized. You start doing this with little things, like organizing your work for school into folders or binders and keeping track of your journals and homework. As soon as you get more organized, you will become more responsible.

Sincerely,
B.T. Menaugh

P.S. I talked with Mr. Lanza last Monday, and I told him that you've been working really hard the last couple of days, so he agreed with me on giving you a day off of school, so this Friday you don't have to come to school. Isn't that great? Others may call it Veteran's Day, but you will know it's Juan Appreciation Day.

Dear Vicky,

Don't worry, it's not hard to be a good leader. You have to be yourself, but don't think of yourself first. Help others before you do anything else. To be a good leader, you have to be strong and outspoken.

You are already an inspiring person. You go to school, work, and care about your future and family. I'm proud of you.

Love,

Amy

The above examples will probably make it clear that this process will bring some pretty good (and perhaps funny!) advice from your own brain. You'll have to decide whether you're "heroic" enough to follow it!

Chopra, D. & Chopra, G. (2011). *The seven spiritual laws of superheroes: Harnessing our power to change the world*. New York, NY: HarperOne. (Original work published 1994)

Fallon, J. (2011). *Thank you notes*. New York, NY: Grand Central Publishing.

Files, M. (2016). *Writing what you know: How to turn personal experiences into publishable fiction, nonfiction, and poetry*. New York, NY: Allworth Press.

THANKS FOR OPENING YOURSELF

Hopefully the work you created from the invitations on these pages has left an afterglow. Continue to use the tools you felt were most helpful and keep honoring your words in ways that exercise your brain and stretch your thinking. Perhaps you'll return to the hero letter when life throws you a situation that calls for good advice. May you continue to find ways to express gratitude to others as you grow in understanding and confidence through your writing.

— MP and KS

UP
TO NEON WORDS.

We'd like to thank those who have informed or contributed to these pages:
Gerry Barton, Gayle Brandeis, Roxanne C., Indrawati D.,Neva Daniels, Ann Dernier, Judy Dyl, Sergio E., Jimmy Fallon, Meg Files, Hannah Gomez, Veronica G., Vicky H., Larry Hammer, Juanita Havill, Juan L., Katie M., Ashley McDonald, Quinn McDonald, Christopher McIlroy, B.T. Menaugh, Marianna Neil, Terry Owen, Jesus P., Mary Ellen Palmeri, Dr. Marianna Pegno, Steve Pellegrino, Pima County Public Library Staff, Charline Profiri, Staff of Raging Sage, Carlie Ricketts, Roger Sather, Irma Sheppard, Janni Simner, Siraaj, Barbara Stahura, Donna Steiner, Jennifer J. Stewart, Lynne Weinberg, Leigh Allison Wilson, Dr. Lucy Wilson.

Special thanks to our partners at Magination Press, including Kristine Enderle, who believed in this book; Vallen Driggers, whose vision made it strong; Melissa Jane Barrett, who made it beautiful; and Katie Ten Hagen, who jumped in when duty called!

ABOUT THE AUTHORS

Marge Pellegrino is a teaching artist who facilitates writing and expressive arts workshops in schools, libraries, and community settings. Her books include *Too Nice*, *My Grandma's the Mayor*, and the award-winning *Journey of Dreams*. She co-wrote *The Sculpture Speaks: A Refugee's Story of Survival*, which supports the work of the Owl & Panther program for refugee families impacted by torture and traumatic dislocation. Marge lives in Tucson, Arizona. Visit MargePellegrino.com and Facebook.com/marge.pellegrino.

Kay Sather is an experienced designer, illustrator, editor, and freelance writer. She's currently finishing a book about the hand-sculpted mud guesthouse she built in her desert backyard. Kay lives in Tucson, Arizona.

ABOUT MAGINATION PRESS

Magination Press is an imprint of the American Psychological Association, the largest scientific and professional organization representing psychologists in the United States and the largest association of psychologists worldwide. Visit maginationpress.org.